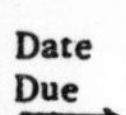




**Nadler, Paul S**

Paul Nadler writes about banking, by Paul S. Nadler. Written for and published by Girard Bank. [Philadelphia] 1972.

73 p. illus. 22 cm.

1. Banks and banking. I. Girard National Bank of Philadelphia. II. Title.

HG1601.N32 332.1′0973 78-189128
MARC

Library of Congress 72

# Paul Nadler writes about Banking

# Paul Nadler writes about Banking

*by Dr. Paul S. Nadler*



*Written for and published by Girard Bank • February 1972*

DR. PAUL S. NADLER, *Professor of Business Administration at Rutgers University, is an internationally recognized authority on banking. Widely known for the understanding, perception and humor that he can bring to complicated financial and monetary subjects, Dr. Nadler has had a distinguished career as teacher, lecturer, author, speaker. He has been teaching undergraduate and graduate students in the fields of banking and international finance for over twenty years, and has addressed more banking conventions and meetings in the past decade than any other American speaker.*

*Dr. Nadler is a consultant to many banks and corporations, the author of many articles on banking including a regular column in the AMERICAN BANKER, and a lecturer at the Stonier Graduate School of Banking.*

*Dr. Nadler is a graduate of Brown University and holds degrees from the University of Wisconsin and New York University. He resides in Summit, New Jersey.*


Library of Congress catalog number: 78-189128
Printed in the United States of America

# Contents

*"If any new ideas come up while I'm out, my vote is 'No!' "*

# Bankers, Good Guys? Bad Guys?

MANY PEOPLE fear and distrust banks. There is a belief that bankers are too powerful, that they control too much of our economic life, that they run almost everything.

Yet banks in the United States are forbidden by law from owning the stock of most businesses. This is unlike many nations, where bankers do indeed control the fabric of business activity. Indeed, banking is America's most regulated industry.

Then why the fear and distrust?

Although banks cannot own businesses, they do have the funds that business needs to borrow. To some, the new golden rule appears to be "He who provides the gold, makes the rules." Thus banks do control business in a negative way by limiting what borrowers can do after they borrow. Nobody likes the man he owes money to—especially when that man intervenes in the business because he worries a lot about getting his money back.

Further, people dislike the banker's conservatism. Banking's motto has long been "never do something the first time," with the modern bankers saying, "You have to do everything a first time—but not now." Thus savings banks got started because banks wouldn't take savings; savings and loan associations got started because banks wouldn't make mortgages; and finance companies got started because banks wouldn't make personal loans. Banking has changed, but a poor reputation takes a long time to live down.

Finally, many people feel that bankers think only of profit rather than of social goals in planning their loans and investments. This is a complex question, but some banks are changing in this regard too. Most important, many people think that banks are monopolies that make too much money by charging the public too much for loans. If true, this charge is enough to make anyone a "bad guy" in our society.

Are bankers monopolists? It depends. Some are, some aren't. But the determination is not as simple as it looks. For a monopoly means that the bank has the market to itself and the public has no choice but to patronize the bank on its terms or go away empty-handed.

What makes a monopoly? It is the lack of competition, rather than the size of the bank. The United States has over 13,500 banks, ranging in size from several hundred thousand to over twenty-six billion dollars! Yet two or three billion-dollar giants in one city fighting each other for business give the public a better deal and are far less monopolistic than one small bank protected by state law from having any competitor established in its town.

There are many towns where the banker has an

exclusive franchise, and he decides what kind of credit accommodations will be given. In some of these towns, the banker does not believe in consumer credit. When a man comes to borrow for a car, he is told something like, "Save up until you can afford a car, and meanwhile you can walk." When no other bank is in town and the neighboring banks feel that this man "belongs" to his local bank, and should not be served elsewhere, he is helpless before a real monopoly.

When a giant bank decides to seek other banks' customers by offering lower cost loans, free checking accounts, or new services, this is competition at its best.

State laws sometimes restrict competition because the states do not want banks to fail and lose their depositors' funds. But the fine line between healthy protection of the public's funds and protection that merely sanctions monopolies is a major issue of our day.

Do banks make too much money? You would think so on seeing the grand buildings, and hearing stories of elaborate parties as bankers entertain each other and their customers. If you look at banks and the way bankers dress and live, you would think banking is America's most profitable business. The public certainly thinks so.

Yet bankers must be poor image makers, and possibly poor businessmen too. For bank profits are low—ranking with those of railroads and stone and clay products—down at the bottom of the list of industries ranked by profit.

Were return on capital invested in banking that good, bank stocks would be a popular investment medium—which they certainly have not been in recent years.

Banking thus appears to have the unique talent of looking like a highly profitable industry—profitable enough to earn public resentment—when it really is not. This helps create the "bad guy" image.

Do banks lend only to business?

Once they did. But look at the competition they brought on themselves by their "never do something the first time" attitude. Now banks serve the small man and the large man alike, for one simple reason: business alone cannot provide banking with enough revenue to pay the bills. Bankers thus have to look to every source of income and every type of service. This is why bankers now worry so much about their image and are trying so hard to become friendly.

Bankers are aware of the changing financial needs—with borrowing, checking account and savings deposit business of the small man increasing in importance while big business becomes relatively less important. Thus bankers want to follow the motto "If ten doctors say you're dead, lie down," and serve the small man better. But the "bad guy" image makes it hard to win new friends.

Why can't bankers shake off this image? Part of it is because many bankers and banks really haven't changed except cosmetically. A new facade and lobby perhaps, but a banker who still knows only the word "No" doesn't impress the public.

Part of it is because traditions die hard and today's bankers must live down their fathers' and grandfathers' mistakes.

But a great part of it is because banks' interest rates are frequently pretty high. Here bankers feel they are getting a bum rap. For banks influence interest rates little more than the butcher sets the price of beef. Sure, they have some control, but if beef becomes scarce, the butcher pays more and rations his scarce supplies by raising prices, just as the banker pays the saver more and then also rations scarce funds by raising interest rates.

It's a little more complicated, since banks can expand the money supply to a degree. But basically bankers are middlemen of money just as butchers are middlemen of meat.

What do bankers generally ask? To be called "good guys?" No, they merely ask that all bankers not be tarred with the same brush. Some are good guys to the public, some are bad guys. Acute bankers earnestly seek a public that looks at each bank individually before judging.

Mayor La Guardia in New York City used to say to the reporters, "Be sure you have your facts *straight* before you distort them."

That's all the banker wants.

VICE PRESIDENT
SMALL LOANS

# Sam, You Made the Rates too High

THE POPULAR SONG of the Twenties, "Sam, You Made the Pants Too Long," might be conversely applied to bank interest rates. Banks are always criticized for high interest rates.

If we recognize that banks are largely middlemen and that interest rates are controlled by supply and demand for funds, we can turn this around and ask why doesn't the government keep money so plentifully available that interest rates are low all the time? This could do the job. For with ample availability of money, no lender could raise his rates. If he did so, the borrowers would go elsewhere.

But do we really want this?

It would be easy for the government to arrange to have plenty of money around all the time. But it is not easy for an economy to produce enough goods and services to match the quantities of money available. Were we to have rapid growth in money supply, but no greater ability to produce goods and provide services, we would simply bid up the prices of the goods and services and get rampant inflation.

Well, what's wrong with inflation?

We have had inflation since the end of World

War II, and the American people have never lived better. Personal income has more than quadrupled since 1945. Virtually every home has at least one television set. We have enough cars to have parking problems in every community. We work fewer hours than ever before, yet we have more to spend for everything. Even our poor live better than the rich of most nations. What's bad about inflation?

First, inflation, like a landslide starts small, but unchecked becomes a disaster. Many remember the German inflation of 1923 when people were paid three times a day so they could spend their money before it lost its value; when people went to a restaurant and found the price of the dinner had doubled after they finished the soup; when people who lived on fixed incomes from interest or rents found that what had been a comfortable annual income now would not pay for a loaf of bread.

The United States has had modest inflation despite the efforts being made to keep prices stable. Were we to accept inflation as part of our way of life, such modest inflation would quickly become a runaway inflation, for everyone would want to spend his money immediately before it lost value, and this would bid prices out of sight.

Thus, acceptance of inflation would lead to boom and bust—heavy spending now, and then a sharp depression when people had overbought everything to beat inflation. This would cost more jobs in the long run than the restraints placed on the economy to prevent inflation from becoming rampant.

Second, even modest inflation has its price. Those who have fixed incomes, such as pensions and insurance, are hurt by the steady erosion of the value of their money. The aged suffer most, and all who have saved for their future are penalized, while those who have borrowed find that inflation steadily eases the burden of the debt. Inflation penalizes the diligent and benefits the profligate.

Why don't we all fight inflation? The answer is that inflation control has a cost. The restraint necessary to stop or slow inflation costs us jobs and markets. This is the dilemma—we can stop inflation at the sacrifice of present jobs and income, or we can maximize jobs by creating enough money to provide work for all. However, this would lead to inflation, followed by boom and bust, and later, even more lost jobs.

It would be nice if we could have the optimum—jobs for all without inflation. But with the various power blocks of the nation and their ability to push wages and prices up even when restraint is severe, such optimum is not possible.

Right now we have government intervention to curb these power blocks temporarily so that inflation can be moderated. But the experience of every free nation shows that the choice remains between full employment at the price of inflation now and lower employment later; or restraint of inflation at the price of fewer jobs and markets now.

What has this to do with the price of money?

One major means of halting inflationary pressures in our country is through restricting the availability of funds. By doing this, the Federal Reserve Board hopes to reduce the demands for goods and services when supplies of them are scarce. If people have less money to spend, the prices of scarce goods will be bid up less rapidly, or not at all.

But since interest rates are the price of money, they follow the rule of all prices—reduced supply means higher prices. Inflation control means less money available and thus higher interest rates.

What is the banker's attitude about all this?

In the dilemma between jobs vs. inflation control, the banker generally favors inflation control. For bankers traditionally have been conservative in their desire for a sound economy and a sound dollar, even if it costs jobs now. This does not improve their popularity. But most bankers believe that a sound economy now and more jobs later are worth the price being paid.

But isn't this a price paid by someone else? Don't banks really gain great benefit from high interest rates? Isn't their concern for inflation control sheer self-interest with a public veneer overlaid on it?

The answer is "Yes and No." A typical economist's answer.

Sure, banks get higher interest rates on loans when the Federal Reserve tightens availability of money, so they earn more. But since banks are middlemen, when they earn more on loans, they must also pay more interest on savings accounts.

Also, banks gain some of their income from the deposit money the Federal Reserve lets them create. When the Reserve Board limits the growth of the money supply, it really limits the growth of bank deposit money. Thus banks earn more on what they lend, but they have less to lend at the higher rates.

Finally, banks have investments that earn fixed income. When interest rates rise, these fixed-income securities are worth less, and the banks take losses on them as they sell them to get money to meet customer needs.

What can we conclude? Some banks benefit from tight money, some don't. But basically tight money is necessary if we are to fight inflation without having the government decide who borrows and spends. The banks serve as the middlemen passing on the Federal Reserve's credit restraint to the public. This doesn't help their image.

However, the banker didn't make the interest rates high—the Federal Reserve decided this.

If you give up smoking, you gain weight. Then when you go on a diet, you develop a twitch. If you're nervous, you're nervous.

Similarly, if power blocks, deficit spending, financing wars and other forces bring about inflation, there is no painless way of stopping it. If Sam hadn't made the rates too high, we probably wouldn't have been able to afford the pants.

*"Would you mind showing me how to kite checks?"*

## Everything But the Printing Press

WE HAVE SAID earlier that banks create money. This does not mean that they own printing presses down in the cellar, and grind out greenbacks to meet daily demand . . . although there was a time when banks literally issued their own currency.

What we call money in the United States or in any other free economy is really a claim against a bank deposit. Certainly we consider cash to be money, but our basic money is really checkbook money, which is nothing other than an order to a bank to debit one account and credit the other.

If I write, "Julie, give Mr. Jones $100" on a piece of paper and tell my daughter to give it to him, he doesn't feel richer. Nor is he. Julie won't do it.

But if I write on a piece of paper, "Girard Bank: Give Mr. Jones $100," and give it to Mr. Jones, and my account is at Girard, then he is $100 richer . . . if I have at least $100 in my account. For Girard will honor this, since this is what a bank check says.

Such claims on bank accounts normally moved through the medium of a bank check, constitute the basic money of the United States, and finance nine-tenths of all transactions.

When someone comes in to borrow money from a bank, the loan, if granted, represents the creation of new money by the bank.

If the borrowing simply involves the bank's adding to the account of the borrower, the bank has automatically created deposit money.

If the borrower asks for cash and the person who receives it from the borrower when he spends it puts the cash back in the bank, then the bank has created new deposit money.

If the borrower gets a bank official check and spends it, the check goes to someone else who deposits it in his account, and again new money has been created. The check was nothing but a piece of paper before the banker signed it, but now it has given someone a new deposit. Thus, when people borrow from the banks, banks create money.

The question that is immediately raised is whether or not banks should be allowed to create all this money simply by signing pieces of paper.

That is where the Federal Reserve System comes in. It limits banks in their ability to create this money. And were it not for its controls, commercial banks could create unlimited deposit money and we could have inflation that would boggle the mind.

So control over borrowing is exercised by the Federal Reserve Board. This control is exercised by requiring the banks to hold cash reserves and to keep deposits in their regional Federal Reserve Bank. The Federal Reserve decides that a bank must keep as a reserve a certain percentage of its total deposits. If the bank does not have enough cash to back new deposits, it can not make new loans, for it is not allowed to hold the new deposits that these new loans would generate. By changing reserve requirements and bank reserves, the Federal Reserve determines how many loans banks can make and how much deposit money they can create.

By controlling the ability of banks to create new deposit money through loans, the Federal Reserve Board helps control inflation. If the Federal Reserve Board wishes to reduce inflation, it limits the ability of banks to create new money. If the Board wishes to encourage economic activity, it allows banks to lend more money by expanding their reserves and thus their ability to create deposit money.

That's how banks create money . . . even without a printing press. And this is one way the economy is regulated in the free market system. This is called monetary policy.

There are other ways of regulating the economy, some of which work with the present system, and some which replace it. Consider first those that work with the present economic system.

Fiscal policy is one method of regulating the economy within the present system. This is the decision that Congress makes when it decides whether to tax more than it spends, and thus withdraw money from the economy, or to spend more than it taxes, and thus add new funds to the economy.

Theoretically, this system calls for the withdrawal of the money from the economy during inflationary time through higher taxes, and pumping money back into the economy during poor times by tax reductions. But, fiscal policy by itself does not achieve its goals of stimulating or contracting the economy. As a corollary to fiscal policy, we need to examine the debt management policy of the Treasury, which helps make fiscal policy effective.

For Congress spends the money and determines tax collections, but if there is a deficit, the Treasury Department has to borrow new money.

If our government is operating with a deficit and the Treasury Department must find more money, they can borrow it from the banks. This creates new money and stimulates the economy. Or the Treasury Department can borrow money from the savings of individuals and business firms by selling types of securities that these groups generally buy. This avoids the creation of new money. Thus the method used by Treasury to secure funds spent by Congress has a direct bearing on business activity.

Monetary, fiscal and debt management policy are the three ways of regulating the economy with maximum freedom for the open market to decide who gets money and who is denied the funds.

Although complicated, this system can work reasonably well if all three phases work together: the Federal Reserve Board's monetary policy, the fiscal policy of Congress, and debt management policies of the Treasury Department. Unfortunately, these work at cross purposes too often, especially because of our unwillingness to raise taxes and cut government spending when economic conditions make these policies desirable.

There are other means of regulation, but these involve a much greater degree of governmental intervention. A drastic approach is direct control by the government—telling people what they can and cannot do, what they can and cannot buy, and what the goods will cost.

Another type of government control being used at present is called "incomes policy." Incomes policy involves governmental intervention to help decide what the prices should be, and what the wage levels should be in the economy. It is used when the power of business and labor groups exceeds the controls that the government can wield through monetary, fiscal and debt management policy.

Incomes policy, therefore, involves giving up some of our free market decision-making for the advantages that come from having a more certain control over the specific sectors that cause inflationary pressures. Because we have lived as a free nation for so long and enjoyed the benefits of free markets, a peace-time incomes policy is almost impossible to sustain without changing our entire social and economic structure. Most of us hope that incomes policies remain temporary and mild.

The control over our economy through monetary

policy, fiscal policy and debt management policy gives the banks a considerable role in deciding who gets money and who does not when credit conditions must be tightened to fight inflation. But the United States and many other nations have felt that this bank decision-making with the public bidding for funds is superior to alternatives, because it is most consistent with a free economic system.

It does, however, put the banks on the spot, because of the key role they play in allocating scarce funds when some restraint is necessary.

A few words about debt.

In a country with a background of frugality, debt has always been a dirty word. But is debt bad?

There is the popular notion that rising debt is automatically bad. Most people worry about rising individual debts, rising business debts, and especially, rising public debts.

However, we cannot live without debt. For an economy to grow, savings must be invested. This means that someone must borrow the funds held in insurance, pensions, time deposits and other savings forms. If the public wants to save more, the debt of individuals, business and the government must rise. Thus, debt by itself is necessary. Otherwise, the savings that some people take out of the spending stream would not come back into circulation. We need debt just as much as we need savings. The main concern is the soundness of the debts.

Most banks spend a minimum of five years to

train lending officers. This seems ridiculous. I could train a man to lend money in ten minutes. Banks will admit this is true. Loan officers can be trained to lend money in ten minutes, but it takes banks the rest of the five years to train them to lend it so they can get it back.

Banks and other lenders cannot stay in business if they create unsound debt. This ability to repay is what we worry about—not the quantity of debt.

Another concern is national debt. Many worry because it is rising and amounts to $2000 for every man, woman and child in the United States.

Yet we can afford this debt because our savings are growing rapidly too. We should look at national debt as a valuable residual, increasing when people do not want to borrow the savings of others, decreasing when people want to borrow more than the amount of savings in the nation.

If rising national debt can serve as a balance wheel . . . providing the offset to savings, and providing the added borrowing that can keep people and resources at work without inflation . . . this is good. But when national debt grows, and we do not have the resources available to match this new borrowing and spending, we get inflation. This is bad.

Thus, there is nothing intrinsically wrong with debt. Without debt there could be no growth. But it must be sound and manageable, and our national debt should be moving in a direction consistent with the best interests of our people and resources.

*"I do appreciate a friendly welcome."*

## Who Watches the Banks While the Banks Watch You?

BANKS MAY BE REGULATED, and their power to create deposit money may be controlled by the Federal Reserve, but bankers still are on the defensive. For despite the power of banking in our nation, we still allow banks to be private enterprises, chartered by groups of individuals, and operated by them for their own personal profit.

Should so important an industry as banking be left to private owners whose basic goal is their own profit?

What are the alternatives? In the United States, we have a few banks owned by labor unions that try to make loans conducive to the union's goals. But basically, the alternative would have to be government ownership of banks.

On the surface, government ownership of banks would appear preferable to private ownership, for it would take the decision of allocation of funds and the granting of loans away from bank officers, and turn it over to the government. However, there are many drawbacks to this scheme.

The first is philosophical in nature. In the United States, we have been led to believe in the free market system. Despite its many faults, it has still proven to be the most successful economic system devised. Under it, our country has grown and prospered for nearly 200 years, giving our citizens an abundance of freedom and prosperity.

A basic building block in the free market system concerns the allocation and distribution of funds. Under the present system, funds are generally made available to those able to pay the highest price for them, all other things being equal. Were we to have government ownership of banks, this system of market decision-making would be replaced by political decision-making, with the government exercising complete determination regarding the allocation of funds to industries, companies and even individuals.

Although many people feel that this would achieve more of our social goals, most fear that political motivations, regardless of how desirable they might be, would distort the economy to a much greater extent than the free market system. The power to grant loans, placed in the hands of government bureaucrats, would create an overriding power in the hands of the government.

When the highest bidder obtains the funds, lower yielding areas such as housing frequently become the victims. Unfortunately this often occurs when money flow must be restricted in order to reduce inflationary pressures. In a sense, this penalizes the lower socio-economic groups at a time when their needs might be the greatest. Even recognizing this, it would seem that the placement of vast new financial powers in the hands of an already all-powerful government would substantially change our economic system.

Further, in times of inflation, the government would be faced with placing the same restrictions on itself that it now places on banks, so that even governmental ownership of banks offers no solution to social problems.

For these reasons, the United States has let the private banking system survive. However, many believe that modifications in the bank's ability to utilize funds, placing greater emphasis on social goals and providing incentives to serve areas such as housing, would be most desirable.

But this does not mean that banking's activities go unwatched. There are many restraints, but they are basically to protect your money.

The number of banks allowed in any community is limited by government. Persons wanting to start a bank or open a branch must first get a charter from the Federal Government or the state, depending on whether it is to be a National or State Bank.

It must prove that the public convenience will be served by the establishment of this bank and that no present bank will be harmed too severely by the new institution or branch.

This is done to avoid cutthroat competition that could cause one or more banks to fail.

In any other industry nobody would care. If a

grocer goes bankrupt, people say it's his problem. But when banks fail, they lose everyone's money.

Banks have their own money invested in themselves. This is called capital. If a bank fails, this money is lost first. And the Federal Deposit Insurance Corporation protects deposits up to a certain amount (now $20,000). But when a bank goes under, it can well lose more than the owner's capital, and many individuals frequently have more than the insured amount in their accounts. Thus, innocent people suffer from a bank failure.

The dilemma of regulators is to protect banks from cutthroat competition, but not protect them so much that there is no competition. This is a fine line to walk.

Banks are also supervised in the types of loans and investments they can make in order to safeguard the money on deposit with them. When a bank has created a deposit by making a loan, someone owns that deposit—either the borrower or the person who got the money spent by the borrower—and the owner counts on his money being there. Banks are watched because all their money except for a modest amount of capital is owed to some depositor.

That's why a banker can't be allowed to make slipshod loans. He's using someone else's money.

Banks are also examined periodically to make sure that they actually have the assets they say they have.

The examiners come in, unannounced, and audit

several areas of the bank. They make sure that cash on hand matches the bank's records, that investment securities and loan agreements on hand are those the bank reports it has, that the loans are being repaid on time. Many other audits are used to make sure that the bank is sound.

In addition, banks are watched to make sure that they do not become too powerful and that the United States does not suffer from excess concentration of banking assets in too few hands.

This is done in part through the restrictions on the number of branches a bank may have, with the regulators making sure that one bank does not play too important a role in any one section of the community. It is also done by restrictions on the merger of banks—with the Justice Department and the bank regulators allowing two banks to merge only when they feel it is in the public interest.

Finally, it is done in some states by the laws that limit banking so that a bank can have no branches and must operate entirely within one building. Many observers feel this is excessive caution at the expense of efficient banking, and that it often leads to local monopolies instead of more competition. However, it is intended to prevent excess concentration of banking assets in that state.

The result is that banking is watched to make sure every bank is safe and that the public gets the best banking service possible.

If we regulate banks so carefully, why do we

need deposit insurance too?

Remembering that we use deposit money for most of our transactions by writing checks, and that banks can create deposit money when people get loans, this means that banks count on people wanting to hold and spend deposit money instead of turning it all in for currency issued by the Federal Reserve.

When a bank makes a loan, it creates a deposit. The holder of that deposit can come in and ask for currency, and the bank has to give it to him. When a man brings a check to the bank, the bank can't tell him to wait while it sends a teller across the street to cash it at the A & P.

Banks keep some currency on hand, but obviously they do not keep everything in currency form. First of all, they do not have that much cash—since they only need about one dollar of cash or reserves for each seven or eight dollars on deposit. Secondly, if all deposits were held in cash, they would not have lent any money out. The bank then would have no income, and the community would get no loans.

If everyone came into the bank at once to turn his deposits into currency, no bank would have enough currency on hand to meet these withdrawals, and the bank could readily fail.

But people do not normally require their funds in currency. As long as they have confidence in the bank and know it will not fail, they do not demand currency and the system can work. Federal

Deposit Insurance is simply a means of guaranteeing that the depositor will, within legal limits, get his money back—so that no panic withdrawals of currency will develop.

As long as we are willing to accept bank deposits as money, the bank can expand the money supply when the Federal Reserve lets it do so to meet growing money needs in the nation. If we all accept something as money, then it serves as money. And deposit insurance gives us the final confidence to accept bank deposits as money.

The result is that when demands for funds grow, and the creation of new money to meet these demands will not cause inflation, the Federal Reserve lets the banks expand the supply of deposit money to meet demand.

So what if our money comes from private banks instead of the government? There are plenty of government people watching to make sure our money is safe, and the system works. What more do we need?

*"How much would the tax be if I leave it ALL to the Government?"*

# God Bless You, Mr. Patman

WHY SHOULD A BOOK commissioned by a bank applaud the banking system's severest critic?

Congressman Wright Patman of Texas has long been the most vocal opponent of banking power in Congress. His opposition to banks and to banking operations is well known throughout the country. Many wonder why Mr. Patman has selected banks for his continuing and unremitting criticism.

Some believe it is because Mr. Patman is a Populist who still looks upon the United States as a country that should be composed of small, individual business and labor units such as we had in the 19th century. To many people, the prospect of dealing with small, personalized business entities rather than giant corporations is most appealing. And banking appears to reflect the growth in power that Mr. Patman opposes.

However, as much as we might like the idea, the day of the small farmer, the small lender, the small corner grocery store, the small bank is passing into American history. We all shop at big supermarkets where thousands of items are available for purchase. Our food is grown on giant "factory-farms." Our automobiles are spewed out of gigantic factory complexes capable of turning out a car a minute. Indeed, nothing is done on a small scale any longer.

As a Populist, therefore, Mr. Patman appears to be fighting for a way of life that is just not here anymore. And since commercial banks reflect the changes in business activity, many believe that Congressman Patman looks upon them as typifying the changes in American life.

Another reason for Mr. Patman's opposition to banks is his great concern for more and better housing. Many Congressmen believe that commercial banks do not place sufficient emphasis on home loans in the way that other financial institutions do —notably savings and loan associations.

Mr. Patman is correct. Many commercial banks do not emphasize mortgage loans. Other outlets for funds are far more profitable. This is why other lending institutions have also de-emphasized mortgages and pushed for broader lending authority.

However, banks do finance the state and local governments which provide for the communities where homes, schools and other such facilities are located. And banks finance the business firms that create the materials used to construct the homes, and finance the appliances and furnishings for them.

Nevertheless, Congressman Patman has a point. Our bankers should be able to provide a greater amount of mortgage money to solve the critical housing needs of the nation, without taking too great an income sacrifice or risk of loss. Unfortunately, most bankers oppose Mr. Patman's proposals without examining their justification.

Mr. Patman has fought strenuously to force banks to report on the disposition of Trust Department funds. In this respect, he is right. Bank Trust Departments manage and invest tremendous wealth and the public deserves the right to know how and where this wealth is being invested in the fabric of the American economy.

The representative from Texas also leads the fight to break up interlocking directorates under which many men serve as directors or officers of savings and loan associations or mutual savings banks and competing commercial banks.

Since the public is best served by independent financial institutions that compete vigorously for the public's business through offering lower rates and better service . . . the continuation of interlocking directorates is inimicable to public welfare. It is impossible for man to serve two masters, or two competitive institutions. Mr. Patman's fight to eliminate interlocking directorates is to be commended.

Congressman Patman's views with respect to the Federal Reserve System also bear close examination by bankers and the public. Many agree with his complaint that the Federal Reserve Board is too independent. Many agree that there is danger in permitting the Federal Reserve Board to make major decisions with regard to availability of credit and the welfare of the country without being subject to Congressional review and control. Many fear that this places the Federal Reserve in the status of "super agency" . . . playing a dominant role in our lives and yet independent of the peoples' will.

This is a very complicated issue. Monetary policy must be independent of politics, if the country is to gain the restraints needed, no matter how politically unpopular those restraints might be.

On the other hand, there are ample reasons to question whether the Federal Reserve Board should be completely independent of the will of Congress, barring such drastic action as congressional willingness to change the Federal Reserve Act. It would seem that the power of the Federal Reserve Board to regulate our economy should be subject to some moderate restraint and control.

Congressman Patman's suggestion that the term of the Chairman of the Federal Reserve Board be the same as that of the President of the United States would seem to be a good start towards the solution of the problem. This would permit greater coordination between the Administration and the Reserve Board and should promote a healthier economy.

His proposal that the accounts of the Federal Reserve Board be audited by the Federal Government also makes sense. Since this is a quasi-government body, such an audit would seem to be in the best interests of the public. But beyond this, Federal Reserve independence is vital for sustainable economic growth.

The greatest area of disagreement that one can hold with Congressman Patman is his demand that interest rates be kept low at all times in order to aid the small borrower. While one can applaud these aims, the practical application is questionable.

High interest rates are not a plot. They are not a conspiracy among banks or between banks and the Federal Reserve Board. Rather they result from the demand for funds vastly exceeding supplies. To provide everyone with all the money wanted at low interest rates when goods are not widely available would result in major inflation. It would penalize those who had saved money and counted on its value remaining strong . . . and would benefit those who had borrowed and could thus pay back in cheaper dollars. We would be rewarding the grasshopper at the expense of the squirrel.

On balance, bankers should bless Congressman Patman! Banking has tremendous power in the communities it serves, and needs a "conscience" to prevent the misuse of such power. In a sense, Congressman Patman speaks for all of us on many issues and we should expect our institutions to respond to such issues. Although some of his proposals are impractical, if not impossible, much of what he says bears careful examination and thoughtful comment by the bankers. Were there no Mr. Patman, banking might be well advised to invent one.

*"Jones certainly took that merchandising course seriously."*

## If You're Worth 5% at 90 Days, Why Nothing on Demand?

MANY WONDER WHY banks don't pay interest on demand deposits. There's a good answer: It is illegal.

Consider the banker's dilemma. Every loan or investment that the banker makes results in a combination of risk, income and liquidity. Risk is the chance of losing money. Income is the return for lending money. Liquidity is the ability to convert an asset quickly into cash when necessary without undue loss. You get one. You lose another. You can't have an investment that gives highest yield with maximum liquidity and no risk of loss.

Banks have to keep a large part of their demand deposit proceeds liquid because money has to be available to be paid out on demand.

There is the story of the man who wrote a check, only to have the bank return it to him stamped "Insufficient Funds." When he called to complain, saying that he had far more money in the bank than he needed to cover the check, the banker replied, "When we stamp Insufficient Funds, it may mean that *you* have insufficient funds, or it may mean that *we* have insufficient funds."

This is obviously only a story, for if a bank did this once, it would not have many customers left the next day.

The conclusion is that a bank must consider liquidity very important when using the demand deposit balances its customers leave.

Before 1933, banks were allowed to pay interest on checking accounts. Consequently, they had to meet the high cost of paying such interest in addition to all of the other costs involved in handling checking accounts. Therefore, in order to obtain sufficient income to operate without sacrificing too much liquidity, they had to accept high-risk loans. This hurt the solvency of the banks. To this day, many believe that this was a major contributor to the failure of half of the banks in the United States in the early thirties. As a result, after 1933 the government ruled that commercial banks could not pay interest on checking accounts. In a sense, no interest on checking accounts means more security for depositors.

That's why interest is not paid on demand deposits.

On the contrary, many banks charge their customers for maintaining checking accounts. One would think that banks earned so much money from using their customers' checking account funds that they could well afford to give checking services away free. Unfortunately, this is not usually so.

It costs the bank somewhere in the neighborhood of $40.00 just to open up a checking account. In addition, the handling of paper and services in the American economy has become a super-expensive animal. Many banks have found that they simply cannot afford to handle some checking accounts unless service charges are assessed.

Many people complain that the service charges are applicable mainly to small accounts and that small depositors pay a disproportionate price for checking services.

This is not always true. Large companies also pay service charges when their deposit balances do not earn enough for the bank to cover the cost of handling the account. But most of the time it is true, because bank costs relative to income are highest on the smaller accounts.

In a great many cases, however, banks offer low or no service charge accounts even if they cause small losses, in order to attract checking account deposits on the theory that the small man today might be the big man tomorrow. Such action has the tendency of driving down the service charges leveled by all banks. This is another way in which a number of banks competing with one another in a community serves the public well.

One other main complaint against banks is that they not only assess service charges for accounts, they make it pretty difficult to get a check cashed if you don't have an account at the bank.

Let's examine the banker's viewpoint.

First, if he cashes a check for someone, and it turns out that the casher was not the rightful owner, the banker is liable for the loss.

Second, even when the right person cashes it, the bank still has the cost of clearing the check to get it back to the bank it was written on in order to get its money back. This cost not only includes the record keeping, photographing for records, and shipping costs, it also includes the loss of the use of the money to the bank during this process.

When a bank cashes a check, it gives out currency—and until it gets the money back from the bank on which the check was written, it loses the use of the money and the interest the money could earn if it were loaned out or invested. This could take two days or more.

Big deal? Consider the loss of the use of funds for two days. What is hard to grasp is that banks handle millions, and loss of the use of $1 million for only two days costs a bank over $300, when interest rates are 6 percent.

The use of money is expensive. When the State of Alaska sold its oil drilling rights, it chartered a jet to fly the checks it received to New York and Chicago—because it cost less to charter a jet from Alaska to New York than the State would have lost in interest by sending the certified checks on a regular flight and having them arrive to be deposited one day later.

This loss of interest income as time passes works

two ways, though. The public has also learned how expensive money is and what its "time value" is. As a result, fewer and fewer individuals and businesses keep excess funds in checking accounts earning no interest. Rather they move them to time and savings deposits that must pay interest by law when checking accounts can't.

Thus bankers find themselves forced to compete aggressively for 5 percent time and savings deposit money, when they used to live on demand deposit funds. True these checking account dollars had a higher handling cost and a need for more liquidity, but they also came free of interest payments.

However commercial banks are not permitted to offer as much interest for time and savings deposits as other savings institutions can. This is the law. As a result, a great deal of money flows to savings banks and savings and loan associations instead of to the commercial banks.

Why do we have such laws?

First, commercial banks can offer a wider variety of financial services to the public, ranging from demand deposits to savings accounts to installment loans to business loans to trust services. Consequently, such banks have a tremendous advantage in terms of convenience when competing for funds. And the public apparently is quite happy with "one-stop" banking.

Further, commercial banks have more short term loans and investments than savings banks and savings and loan associations do because commercial banks are permitted to hold a variety of assets. Savings institutions are required to place most of their available funds into long term home mortgages.

Since most bank loans are paid off in a short period of time, if interest rates are rising the commercial bank can take this money and relend it at the new, higher interest rates immediately. But the savings bank or savings and loan association is stuck with a long term mortgage at a fixed interest rate, and cannot get most of its money back for several years. Thus, if rates are rising it is stuck with assets that earn less on average than the commercial bank assets earn.

Were commercial banks allowed to pay as much interest as they could afford to pay the public in periods when interest rates are rising, they could outpay the savings and loan associations and savings banks, and the higher bank rates plus the one-stop banking convenience would draw much of the money out of these other thrift institutions. This could conceivably put these other institutions out of business.

The depositor who wishes to save in commercial banks, therefore, is denied the right by law to get as high a return from his savings as he could obtain from a savings bank or savings and loan association. This seems unfair to depositors.

But from the viewpoint that the nation wants to keep all its financial institutions strong to protect the public's funds in them, this restriction on the commercial banks also protects the public.

One can hope, though, that in time we will help these specialized thrift institutions positively instead of negatively. For instead of restricting the interest rates that the commercial banks can pay the saver, the public would be better served if we let the other institutions expand their spheres of operation—so they could compete more effectively with commercial banks in tight money periods. All that banks should ask is that these other institutions be subject to the same handicaps that banks face—notably reserve requirements and the same level of taxes. Otherwise, commercial banks have nothing to fear from a fair fight for savings that would allow each type of institution to pay the public the most it could afford.

If we really believe in free markets, the ceilings on savings rates should eventually be removed. For if the use of money is so expensive, why shouldn't all savers benefit?

*"He's in charge of selecting new foreign offices!"*

## Are Eurodollars for Ameropeans and Stuff Like That?

TODAY MORE AND MORE people hear about Eurodollars, devaluation, exchange rates and terms like these. For we find ourselves involved deeper and deeper in the intricacies of international finance.

What is involved?

The best way to start is to explain that—except for currency—*money* never leaves the country of origin. Only the *ownership* does. Certainly, people can leave the United States and take dollar bills with them, but for large transactions, the basic money used is bank deposit money. And a dollar of bank money consists of a deposit in an American bank. That dollar always stays in American banks, for otherwise the deposit dollar doesn't exist.

Then what moves as we shift funds from country to country? Basically, what happens is that the ownership of the money moves from people in one nation to those in another nation.

Let's take an example: a Frenchman sells wine in the United States and is paid with a check on the wine importer's bank—payable in dollars. Since the French winemaker wants French francs, he sells that check to his bank for a franc deposit or currency. The check now becomes the property of the French bank. To complete the transaction, the French bank sends the check to the United States for deposit in its account at the American bank it deals with.

What has happened, then, is that the ownership of the deposit dollars has moved from the American importer to the French bank—but the money has stayed in United States banks. Only the ownership has moved.

To make it clear, if both the importer and the French bank receiving the check used the Girard Bank, the whole transaction would be completed on the books of Girard right in Philadelphia. Yet ownership of dollars would have moved from an American to a Frenchman.

Later, when some Frenchman wants to buy an American machine tool, he goes to his French bank to get dollars. If it is the same bank, the bank will take his francs and give him a draft—which is like a check. This, in effect, gives him part of that bank's dollar deposit in the Girard Bank. As the Frenchman pays for the tools, his draft goes to the tool seller, and the money is deposited in the American's account at Girard, or at some other United States bank.

In this way we can have international transactions even though the dollars stay in the United States and the francs stay in France.

What then has been the role of gold?

If the French sell more to the United States than Americans sell to France, after a while the French banks own more dollars than they feel they will need to meet the demands of French people who want dollars to buy American goods.

Not wanting to hold dollars forever, the French bank would sell them at a lower price to get rid of them, if necessary. But since the French Central Bank (like our Federal Reserve) wants to keep the price of francs steady relative to the dollar, it would buy the dollars when no one else wanted them to keep the price of dollars from falling. Then, if the French Central Bank in turn felt it had too many dollars, up until 1968 it was able to sell them to the United States Government for gold.

Gold, then, served as the international money—used to settle accounts when one country spent more in another country than the second spent in the first.

What has happened recently, however, has changed this situation.

For a number of years, the United States has been spending more abroad than it has earned. We have settled these so-called balance of payments deficits partly in gold and partly by the willingness of those nations with balance of payments surpluses to hold more and more dollars.

Foreign central banks held these dollars because of their regard for the United States, and because the dollar is the most useful international currency.

This is due to the broad use of dollars that has developed for settling international debts.

In addition, foreign central banks held dollars because the United States offered so many liquid investment opportunities that the foreign holders of these dollar claims could get a good rate of interest on their dollar holdings. Finally, foreign central banks held dollars because we promised to convert their dollar claims into gold at $35 an ounce at any time.

By 1968, however, it became obvious that our offer to convert dollars into gold at $35 an ounce for foreign government was like a "beware of the dog" sign without a dog. For we had about three times as many dollars held overseas that could be turned in for gold as we had gold available to meet these claims. Thus, in 1968, when a great many nations tried to turn in dollars for gold at once, and we did not have enough gold to meet all the claims that might arise, we suspended payment of gold for official dollar claims.

But since our balance of payments deficits continued unabated, foreigners had no choice but to continue to hold more and more dollar claims, even though they could no longer convert them in to gold. Obviously, they did not want to dump the dollars on the market for whatever price they would bring in local currency.

The foreign central banks could have sold their dollars by asking less and less for them in terms of their own currencies. At some price, individual

French, German, Japanese and other individuals and companies would have been interested in buying the dollars. For cheaper dollars would have given them cheaper American goods. But if foreign companies and individuals bought more American goods because they were cheaper, it would mean less sales of local goods, and thus weaker economic activity in other countries.

Thus, the foreign central banks held more and more dollars, and the dollar claims held by official foreign holders rose to almost five times the amount of American gold available. Consequently foreigners became more and more restless at our continuing deficits.

Finally in fall 1971, the United States and the other nations agreed to do something to stop this situation. The most dramatic step taken was to raise the price of gold, but really the fundamental step was the very change in currency values that the other nations had resisted for years.

The devaluation of the dollar, which in effect meant the raising of the price of gold, by itself did nothing. For all it meant was that henceforth instead of not selling gold at $35 an ounce, the United States will not sell gold at $38 an ounce.

But since the officially supported value of other currencies was allowed to move up against the dollar at the same time, it meant that American goods will become cheaper for foreigners to buy. Our domestic prices will stay about the same, but the foreigners can now buy dollars to pay for these American goods at a lower cost in terms of their own currency. Conversely, Americans find foreign currencies more expensive, and thus they will buy fewer foreign goods.

This can help solve our balance of payments deficits problem. Americans will now buy fewer foreign goods and travel abroad less while foreigners will buy more of our goods and services—evening out the balance of payments imbalance to a degree.

But the fundamental step remains that the United States must become more productive, and must use necessary stabilization tools to keep its prices from rising more rapidly than foreign prices do. Otherwise all we have done is gain a little time, and the payments deficits will become worse again.

Foreign governments still hold many billions of dollars. But all that their continued willingness to hold dollars can do is buy time for the United States. For the world is now looking for a new international money called "paper gold" to replace real gold because of its scarcity, and to replace the dollar to a degree—because dollar supplies available in the rest of the world are determined by our domestic policy and by our balance of payments position. Once the world has a new international money, the willingness of foreigners to hold dollars for long periods will be reduced, giving us far less time to settle our deficits before the dollar has to be devalued again and foreign goods and services become even more expensive for Americans to buy.

Thus we may have some time to relax, but basically a nation with a balance of payments deficit is like a family that spends more than it earns. It can live a while on savings and indulgent creditors, but eventually it must earn more or spend less. This is the problem of the United States.

All right, then, what are Eurodollars?

Even though money never leaves the country of origin, some people want to hold dollars, and they want them in banks instead of cash . . . but *not* American banks in the United States.

Who would want this? First it was the Russians, who wanted American dollars in the late 1950's to buy American goods, but who were afraid that our Government might sometime freeze their accounts if they placed them in American banks.

Later it was international companies that wanted to keep U.S. dollars deposited in banks, but felt they could get higher rates elsewhere than American banks were allowed to pay for savings under the Federal Reserve's interest rate ceilings.

Thus, banks in London and elsewhere began accepting deposits, not denominated in their own currency—but rather in U.S. Dollars—*Eurodollars*. In this way the Russians could keep dollars without having them in the United States. The international companies could keep dollars and still get higher interest returns, since the Federal Reserve cannot set interest rate ceilings in London, Nassau, or other foreign points.

These foreign banks became conduits—accepting Eurodollar deposits and then depositing the dollar checks and drafts received in United States banks themselves. For money never leaves its home country, and the banks accepting Eurodollars had no place else to take the checks they had accepted other than American banks. Naturally they accepted the Eurodollars and paid interest on them because they felt they could lend out their new dollar holdings in American banks to other people at an even higher interest rate than they had paid the Eurodollar depositor.

What has made these Eurodollars of great interest to American banks is that when money has been very tight here, American banks have bought Eurodollars in their London and Nassau offices—paying much more than they were allowed to pay in interest at home. In this way they have obtained money to bring home that they otherwise would not have attracted, because of the interest rate ceilings in this country.

This was not a way for all domestic banks to buy new money and get around the Federal Reserve's tight money policy; for the dollars bought by some American banks in London, Nassau and elsewhere as Eurodollar deposits were physically just checks on other American banks. After all that's what dollars are, except for currency. All that the Eurodollar purchases of the big United States banks did was to attract new holders of checks written on banks all over America to deposit these in the overseas offices of other United States banks. This was because these overseas banks could pay more on their time deposits than banks at home were allowed to pay.

There was no creation of new money—just a recirculation from one American bank to another —through Europe.

To put it another way, the Federal Reserve has been and remains the keeper of the bathtub of credit. It decides how much water will be in the tub . . . and all that the bankers can do with their bidding for deposits, Eurodollars, and anything else is to push the soap around from side to side.

What this proves, though, is that American banking and finance, like American business, has become inextricably wedded to foreign markets and operations. We are no longer an American market, we are a world market. And if the most fruitful path for the soap to take in the tub is to flow through England on its trip from one end of the U.S. to the other, that's the way the suds will flow in the years to come.

*"Have you a stock that will go up in time to let me build a new summer cottage?"*

## Are Banks Trustworthy?

MANY AGREE THAT bankers, like boy scouts, are generally loyal, helpful, friendly, courteous, kind, obedient, cheerful, thrifty, brave, clean and reverent . . . but are they trustworthy?

Many think not. Many think the time has come to spin trust departments away from banks.

This has nothing to do with the integrity of banks. It is just that the trust departments of banks are the "owners" of a very substantial part of the wealth of this country. It has been estimated that nearly $300 billion are held in trusts, pensions and profit-sharing funds by the banks of the United States. This is indeed a goodly sum of money.

Many believe that banks should be divested of these funds . . . that different types of corporations should be set up just to handle trust funds.

Their reasoning is this: Even though the banks do not own the money that is left by trust customers for them to manage, the banks do determine how to vote the stock of the companies they invest in for these people.

The United States has laws that keep banks from owning stock in companies themselves, so that the bank is not tempted to give preference in lending money to the companies whose stock it owns.

Some think that the separation of lending power and ownership should be pushed a step further—with the banks prohibited from even buying stock as the representative of those people who ask the banks to manage money for them.

Whether the bank actually owns the stock or just controls it for a trust customer, they still fear the bank will make preferential loans to the companies whose stock it controls. Also, they feel a bank will be able to do a better job of investing for its trust customers than any other investors can do because of the inside information the bank gets in its capacity as a lender.

There is much to this argument. But the question then becomes, "Who should manage the trust assets of the nation instead?"

If they are handled by insurance companies, brokerage firms, investment advisors, or other financial institutions, wouldn't the same possible conflict of interest develop? And if the United States were to require that managers of trust assets do nothing else, there would be very few trust companies in the country, because managing trusts is not a very profitable service until the operation gets large enough to offset the high cost of paper work and of hiring investment talent.

Thus, were the banks to be prohibited from offering trust services, people in many communities would find themselves left without the opportunity to gain such services without travel to major cities.

A better answer appears to be fuller disclosure of trust department operations, stiff enforcement of laws against the use of inside information, and possibly modification of the power trust departments now have to vote the stock they hold.

But tied in to this is a second basic question, "What should be done with the funds in trust accounts?" Many feel that the funds in trust accounts should be used to promote the social goals of the country.

However, trust accounts are established by those who have worked long and hard to acquire wealth. This doesn't include only rich people. It includes corporations who establish pension funds and profit-sharing plans for their employees, unions with large reserves, foundations, and many persons of moderate means who use bank trust departments to provide for the future of their wives and children.

So the money that is left in trust in a bank or any other institution is a very special type of animal. The bank simply serves as the safekeeper for this money, and is charged with attaining the highest return for trust investments consistent with prudence and security. To divert these funds to social goals sacrificing income on the investment, or entailing high risk, would seem to be quite inconsistent with the purpose for which trusts were created. Indeed, the right to establish trusts and expect that the monies will be properly and securely invested is one of the fundamental rights we enjoy in this country.

There is, however, another side to the issue. For just as banks should not utilize the funds of their trust customers to meet social goals, neither should they utilize those funds to influence the economy in other ways.

The power of the trusts resides not only in the great amount of money held in them, but also in the economic power that can be wielded by them. A very substantial part of a great many major corporations in the United States is literally owned by bank trust departments through their control of the stock for trust customers. Some fear the economic power thus available to banks in the exercise of their voting rights for such stock. For though banks themselves cannot own stock, this back door approach might permit them to control companies anyway.

A major question is, "How does the bank vote the stock it holds in trust?" Many banks almost always vote the stock in favor of management on the theory that as long as the company progresses and makes a reasonable profit, management should be supported. Don't rock the boat. However, by voting exclusively for management, banks often make it practically impossible for others to replace management with more competent, or more socially-oriented people.

In recent years, socially-oriented groups have strongly encouraged banks to vote against management . . . particularly management that can be held responsible for problems of pollution, ecology and other social ills.

This is a very thorny question with much to be said on both sides. Banks, by law, must protect the funds held in trust. To do so encourages prudence and conservatism. On the other hand, banks must recognize the social needs and goals of the community and the nation. Perhaps one solution may be for banks to be required by law to abstain from voting stock in trust entirely so that power cannot be abused in either direction, if it is not feasible to pass the voting rights on to the people for whom the bank's trust department serves. Such a law would put the responsibility on individual shareholders to become more active in voting their stock, otherwise management would find itself with non-voting institutional shareholders and apathetic individual stockholders. This would give management free reign.

In any event, banks will have to be far more in tune with the times in handling the power that comes to them through their trust departments.

*"It's o.k. to be friendly, but don't call him 'Buster'."*

## How Friendly Should Your Friendly Banker Be?

AT THE PRESENT TIME, bankers are criticized more for not rendering greater service to their communities than for almost anything else except high interest rates. Many believe that banks place dividends to stockholders and the safety of funds far above the needs of the community, and the social goals that the community must meet.

Yet first and foremost, the banker must think about his depositors, for he is using money that he doesn't own. If he misuses the money or if it is dissipated through bad investments, the savings of depositors are jeopardized. So the banker has a basic responsibility to safeguard the money of depositors. He also owes his stockholders a return on their investments.

In addition, however, banks do have a responsibility to the community . . . for if the community deteriorates, so will the banks that serve it.

But since the banker is not using his own money, he does not have the right to engage in high risk loans to prove his importance to the community.

Further, the amount of money available for loans is limited. Consequently banks are limited in the loans and investments they can undertake.

This is why many believe that banks really have no right to assume the prerogatives of the government and to decide which social goals should be met and which should not be met. Banks are private institutions, not government bodies, they reason. It would seem best for the government to decide what should be done on a broad basis . . . what social goals should be met, and where the funds should be obtained for meeting those goals.

Even with this extremely strict interpretation of the social goals of banks, most of today's bankers recognize that they must, nevertheless, serve the community and help it survive and grow.

Banks cannot move out of the city and into the suburbs the way people and other businesses can. The bank's charter is for its locality and the banker's future is, therefore, intricately tied to the future of the community itself. Thus, while many observers look at a bank's social goals with a very narrow interpretation, many others feel that banks must establish goals that help the area survive and thrive. This, they feel, is in the long range self interest of depositors and stockholders, and thus of the bank.

This explains why many bankers have taken very forward-looking roles in the area of social responsibilities. Many serve on governmental commissions devoted primarily to improving the welfare of the community itself. Most are usually found in the center of the efforts to rebuild center city cores.

Our central cities were originally built on the transportation lines of railroads and rivers. We now use crossings of superhighways and airports as the basis for our commerce. Hence, there is no automatic need for many cities and, unless central cities are made to be interesting, exciting, efficient places again, there is no economic or other justification for their survival. We have had ghost towns in the past, and could have them again. Banks must help prevent this from happening.

The same is true of rural areas. As people migrate to the cities, other businesses can follow them. But not the banker. He is wedded to the community by his charter and cannot follow his customers to the city or the suburbs. Thus, rural bankers should be leaders in industrial development and rural renewal, if for no other reason than enlightened self interest.

Banking's charitable contributions should be examined in the same light. For again bankers are not using their own money. Here they are using shareholders' funds.

It would be easy for the banker to take his shareholders' money and use it for pet causes that build his personal stature in the community. But this use removes capital funds that otherwise would protect deposits, and it makes the banker into a quasi-governmental authority—deciding which charities deserve support and which do not.

Thus, bank charity should also be judged by

whether it serves the long run interest of the bank.

If contributions can attract people to the community or keep it from deteriorating, this is fine. If they support needed institutions that make the community cohesive and stronger, also fine. But the banker must make sure that each gift serves the bank in the long run. Otherwise he is merely enhancing his own stature with other people's funds.

Basically then, banks are not governments. They are not elected, and the funds they have were left with them for safekeeping and for convenience. A bank is not intended to take upon itself the determination of social goals for the community. This is governmental policy that should be financed with tax dollars. Anything beyond long range self interest appears unwarranted.

Yet this covers a lot of ground. It includes undertaking social goals even if only to make banking attractive to today's youth as a career. For without bright young people entering banking, the industry's future is dim indeed. And youth today looks deeper than the accumulation of profits in deciding what type of work is satisfying.

Government can also help the banker resolve his dilemma between seeking profit for his shareholders and safety for his depositors on the one hand, and meeting the social goals of the community on the other.

There are things that can be done to induce banks to rechannel their funds in a way that would be consistent with the banker's goals of serving the community, depositors, employees, and shareholders. One approach is that of changing the reserve requirements of the bank. This would permit those banks that meet the social goals established by the community to keep less of their money idle in reserves. This would automatically free up funds for use by the community without endangering the structure of the bank itself. However, who decides what the important social goals are?

Another approach would be that of using deposits as a sort of "carrot and stick." Banks that met the social goals established by society would be given a greater share of government deposits. Those that did not, would receive a lesser amount. But again, the problem is basically the same as above: who determines the social goals?

These are the bankers' greatest dilemmas today. But one thing is certain. Long range self interest can cover a lot of ground in a society so in need of urban renewal and improvement in the quality of life. Bankers who completely ignore social goals and concentrate on profits, as in the past, are headed for trouble. Bankers today, faced with their problems—urban, rural and suburban alike—cannot be like the man who sat complacently on the sinking Titanic saying, "Why should I worry, it's not my boat."

If the community dies, the bank dies with it. This provides the basic urgency to the new social goals of banking.

TRAVELERS
CHEQUES
SOLD HERE

# Where Do We Go from Here?

IT IS PROBABLY FITTING to consider some of the mistakes that banks have made in the past . . . for they may give us the perspective needed to form a clearer picture of the future.

Banking has been an unusual industry, demanding a great deal of sophistication from its potential borrowers but offering little of the same itself.

Thus, banks have demanded that borrowers know every element of their cost of doing business, while very few banks have actually known the cost of banking.

Banks have demanded that their clients develop a sophisticated pricing of services to assure that the business that borrows funds will operate profitably and the bank will get its loan money back. Banks, on the other hand, simply display their cost of doing business as banks as best they know them, and then tell their customers to "add a little something for profit to the bank."

Many banks have concentrated on growth in size at the expense of bank profit because it meant special prestige for the bank to be larger than other banks.

This writer remembers a banker who went to a major oil company customer to ask for either a fee or more money on deposit because the account was losing money for the bank. The customer said, "No" and the banker returned empty-handed.

"Why didn't you throw the account out of the bank if it was losing money?" he was asked.

"And lose Schmidlapp Oil? It's one of our major accounts," he responded. Obviously profit has been low on many bankers' lists of goals.

But now the profit squeeze is changing this. Banks have to buy funds they used to get free as demand deposits. They are finally becoming profit-conscious.

Similarly, the law of competition has forced many banks to recognize the fact that they can no longer be just banks, but must meet the full financial needs of the community if they are to grow in a growing economy. The conservatism that kept bankers out of the mortgage market, out of the savings market, out of the consumer credit market and out of many other markets is gradually disappearing.

They still revert to form occasionally, however. One of the mysteries of the 1960's was the vigorous fight that banks waged against the "truth in lending" bill in Congress, even though bankers were the low cost lenders and it was definitely to their advantage to have interest rates revealed to borrowers. That took a special kind of talent! Possibly they feared that the public would learn that "discount" rates on autos were twice as high as they looked.

Yet after the law was passed, the public discovered that it paid much higher interest rates to finance companies and other lending institutions than to banks. It is to be hoped that banks have since learned that saying "no" and fighting change for fear of the unknown can hurt them far more than the truth.

Some bankers are finally becoming market oriented and recognizing that the only limit of what a bank should do in serving a community is the limit of prudence, safety and what regulatory authorities will permit. This helps explain why bankers are trying to get away from the image of being tight-fisted Scrooges and espousing the image of community service. Some Scrooges still exist, however.

It may be a hopeful sign to realize that bankers now recognize that you must grow or die . . . that there is no standing still.

Out of this has come the development of a thing called the "one bank holding company."

Commercial banks have often found themselves at a disadvantage when competing for funds and services with finance companies, savings and loan associations, insurance companies and others. This is because banks are banks, and subject to a body of laws that were written a generation ago.

Since a bank takes the deposits of the people and must safeguard these deposits, examiners and regulators are very wary of letting the banks expand into many services that are not specifically related to banking. Thus, banks have watched other competitors become full financial servicers and expand their markets. In order to compete more effectively, a number of banks finally established what was called the "one bank holding company." In this way, stockholders of the bank become stockholders of a holding company that can own both the bank and other financial institutions that the holding company may acquire. Thus, the bank remains the bank, but the shareholders can diversify.

Since the bank remains an independent organism that is simply owned by the same people who own the holding company, the bank is able to maintain the conservative policies that safeguard the deposits of individuals. On the other hand, the holding company is free to acquire other businesses within the framework of the law. The one bank holding company has been placed under the regulation of the Federal Reserve Board by Congress so that the number and types of companies that it can acquire is quite limited and all are in the financial sphere.

The establishment of the "one bank holding company" system will, nevertheless, permit the offer of a significantly broader array of financial services than ever before. This is certainly a long way from the old policy of never doing something the first time.

Another change is the so-called checkless society.

There is much to say for the checkless society. A major national problem in the United States is paper work and the movement of checks. Every year, we write billions of checks that flow through many different steps in our banking system.

Many bankers, and others, have been investigating methods of getting away from the use of checks for routine transactions by developing methods of automatic payment for certain types of bills.

There is considerable interest in having bills for utilities, department store purchases, gasoline purchases sent to the bank instead of the individual. Under this system, the bank would simply credit the seller and debit the depositor . . . notifying the depositor that the money has been removed from his account. Although this seems to be a very safe, sane and logical solution to paper work, a great many depositors regard their bank account as a sacred entity, as well they should, and are not quite prepared to have money removed from their accounts in this manner.

Something like this is bound to come, however, because the inefficiency of the present system staggers the imagination.

In addition, through the use of credit cards, many are trying to get away from the use of checks and cash for other transactions . . . hotel bills, travel, dining out, etc. There is even talk of the day (now technically feasible) when a shoe store salesman will simply press a set of keys that will instruct the bank automatically to move the money out of the customer's account into the store's account. If the customer is overdrawn, the light will flash "put back the boots."

The problems facing this are numerous. First of all, a great many people do not like the idea of having someone decide that money will be moved out of their account, just like that. They like to have control and the right to examine the bills to see if they are correctly charged before paying them. They like to have the opportunity to challenge before money from their account crosses to someone else's account.

Secondly, many people feel that the automatic payment of bills would rob them of funds too quickly. After all, if you don't have to pay the bill until the end of the month, you can rely on next month's income to pay for today's purchases. So even the most unsophisticated depositor uses "float," the same way many sophisticated corporations do.

Finally, there is the high cost of setting up a wire network to move money around the nation, and the question has arisen frequently as to who will pay this expense. Certainly the consumer will not be interested in paying more for the privilege of having money taken away from him faster.

Nevertheless, some form of the checkless society will have to come because the sheer weight of paper work threatens to engulf us all.

The telephone company has estimated that, if

the dial telephone were not put in and operators had to handle every call, it would take all of the women in the United States over the age of twenty-one to handle all of the calls that are made by the American people today. Obviously, we cannot avoid automation in telephone service if we want to have the type of service we feel we need. Similarly, if we avoid seeking a solution to the paper work problem in banking, we will simply have to write fewer checks since it will take too many people to handle them.

Many fear that credit cards and the checkless society will lead to further depersonalization . . . to the concept of "big brother watching you." There is a tremendous fear that, as more and more transactions move from anonymous cash to credit card transactions, banks and other issuers of credit cards will use the data generated by our spending and personal habits as a means of inducing us to buy things we otherwise would not want. Also, banks could become "big brothers" watching over our every transaction, such as we fear in totalitarian nations.

Unquestionably, this could happen. Great quantities of data about our personal spending patterns, never available before, are now accessible. In fact, there is great protest to the use of such data by motor vehicle bureaus and banks to cross-sell other services and to obtain information about people that was not heretofore available.

Thus, technology can enable the government and major institutions to learn enough about us to serve as our "big brothers." It is up to the American people to make sure that this does not happen and that legislation is adequate to protect privacy, even at the sacrifice of some of the efficiencies that come from computerized data and payment mechanisms.

For the future of banking, we can look to development of an even wider range of financial services. Banks will provide as many depositor needs as can possibly be required including bookkeeping, tax preparation and payment, bill paying and many of the other routine chores that people must do for themselves today.

Banks will also offer more services of an investment nature, services that will enable depositors to utilize their deposits more efficiently.

Banks will offer a much broader range of services to corporations. Indeed, the corporate services offered by banks today will seem to be in their infancy compared to the services that will be provided in the future. Using the computer's logic instead of just its paper handling ability, banks are developing a very broad range of sophisticated financial services that will become increasingly valuable to business and professional organizations.

It is also likely that machine banking will ultimately be used on a widespread basis. Machines have already been developed that can handle the receipt of money and the payment of cash. Such mechanisms will be available twenty-four hours a day, and many of our children will seldom visit the insides of banks in the future.

The wire transfer of money under the checkless society will allow banks to compete with others many miles away. This will add to the pattern of bank versus non-bank competition for the public's business, as each financial institution tries to practice "scrambled finance" to a greater and greater degree by getting into their competitor's fields of endeavor. The public can only benefit from this.

Out of the sheer concern over the community's future, if for no other reason, banking will move farther in the lead in meeting social goals.

The days when the banker's motto was "Never do something the first time" are over. Banking in general will have to change at least as rapidly as any other American industry in the years ahead. And in the forward thinking banks; the change should be electric.

The aware banker of today feels nothing but envy for the young men who will be the banking leaders of tomorrow.